BOB DYLAN
Revisited

BOB DYLAN
Revisited

W. W. Norton & Company
New York · London

Bob Dylan by Gradimir Smudja

First American Edition 2009

For information about permission to reproduce selections from this book, write to
Permissions, W. W. Norton & Company, Inc., 500 Fifth Avenue, New York, NY 10110

For information about special discounts for bulk purchases, please contact
W. W. Norton Special Sales at specialsales@wwnorton.com or 800-233-4830

Manufacturing by Toppan
Production manager: Julia Druskin

Library of Congress Cataloging-in-Publication Data

Dylan, Bob, 1941–
[Songs. Texts. Selections]
Bob Dylan revisited. — 1st American ed.
p. cm.
Summary: "Rendered in striking, explosive graphic form, many of Bob Dylan's most famous
songs illustrated as they've never been before. Mesmerized by the power of his lyrics and
intrigued by the possibilities of translating his powerful, enigmatic personality into art,
thirteen leading graphic artists banded together to create this unusual testament to the
universality and transcendent vision of an American musical genius"—Provided by publisher.
ISBN 978-0-393-07617-2 (hardcover)
1. Popular music—United States—Texts. 2. Dylan, Bob, 1941—Illustrations.
I. Title.
ML54.6.D94S62 2009
782.42164092—dc22

                                                2009015567

W. W. Norton & Company, Inc., 500 Fifth Avenue, New York, N.Y. 10110
www.wwnorton.com

W. W. Norton & Company Ltd., Castle House, 75/76 Wells Street, London W1T 3QT

1 2 3 4 5 6 7 8 9 0

CONTENTS

Cover: Gradimir Smudja
Title page: Jean-Philippe Bramanti
Endpapers: Thierry Murat

Blowin' In The Wind (1962) interpreted by **Thierry Murat**

How many roads must a man walk down
Before you call him a man?
Yes, 'n' how many seas must a white dove sail
Before she sleeps in the sand?
Yes, 'n' how many times must the cannonballs fly
Before they're forever banned?
The answer, my friend, is blowin' in the wind
The answer is blowin' in the wind

How many years can a mountain exist
Before it's washed to the sea?
Yes, 'n' how many years can some people exist
Before they're allowed to be free?
Yes, 'n' how many times can a man turn his head
Pretending he just doesn't see?
The answer, my friend, is blowin' in the wind
The answer is blowin' in the wind

How many times must a man look up
Before he can see the sky?
Yes, 'n' how many ears must one man have
Before he can hear people cry?
Yes, 'n' how many deaths will it take till he knows
That too many people have died?
The answer, my friend, is blowin' in the wind
The answer is blowin' in the wind

How many roads ?

How many oceans ?

All that I know, the wind whispered to me.

How many wars?

How many times?

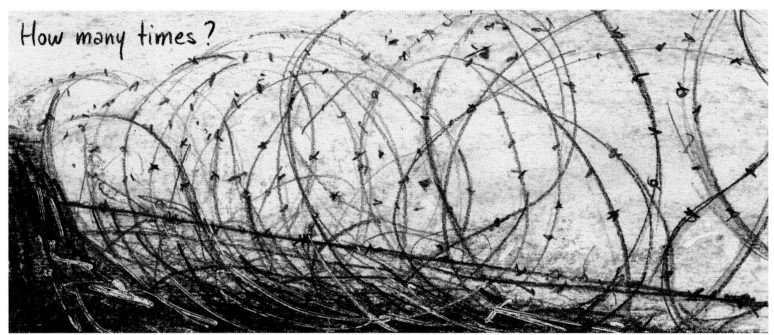

All that I know, the wind whispered to me.

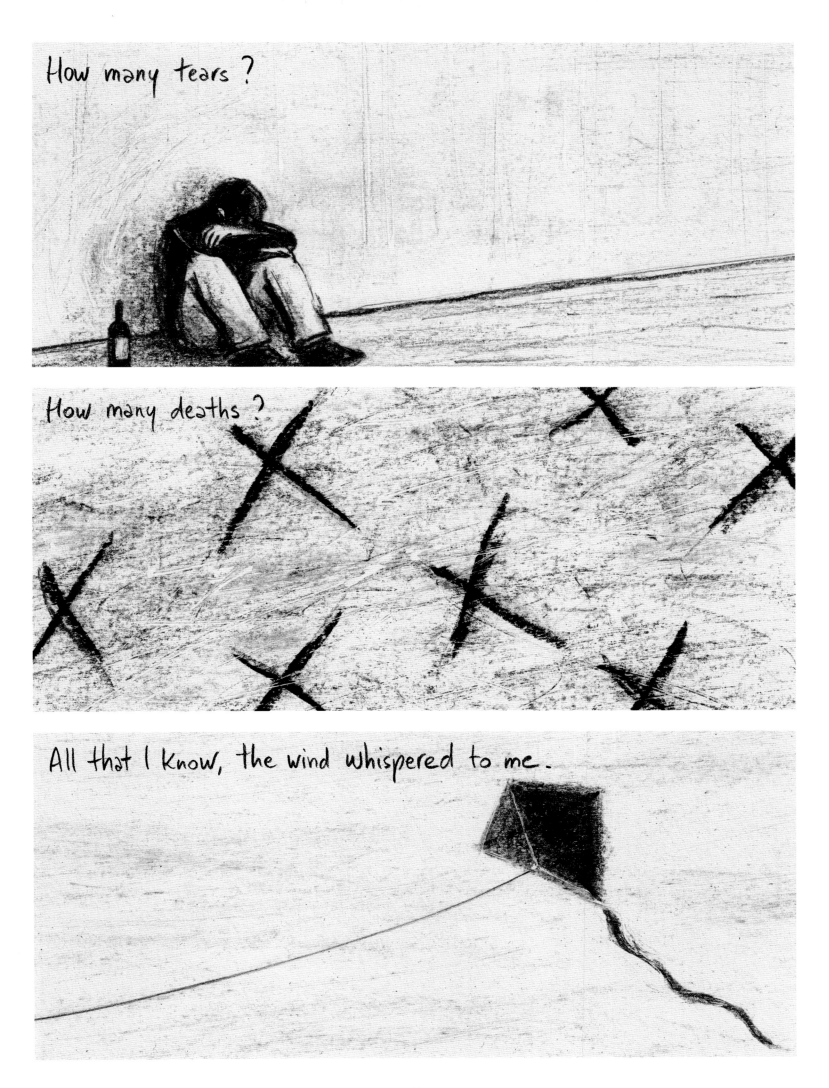

How many years?

How many centuries?

All that I know, the wind whispered to me.

How many questions ?

How many answers ?

All that I know, the wind whispered to me.

A Hard Rain's A-Gonna Fall (1963) interpreted by **Lorenzo Mattotti**

Oh, where have you been, my blue-eyed son? / Oh, where have you been, my darling young one? / I've stumbled on the side of twelve misty mountains / I've walked and I've crawled on six crooked highways / I've stepped in the middle of seven sad forests / I've been out in front of a dozen dead oceans / I've been ten thousand miles in the mouth of a graveyard / And it's a hard, and it's a hard, it's a hard, and it's a hard / And it's a hard rain's a-gonna fall

Oh, what did you see, my blue-eyed son? / Oh, what did you see, my darling young one? / I saw a newborn baby with wild wolves all around it / I saw a highway of diamonds with nobody on it / I saw a black branch with blood that kept drippin' / I saw a room full of men with their hammers a-bleedin' / I saw a white ladder all covered with water / I saw ten thousand talkers whose tongues were all broken / I saw guns and sharp swords in the hands of young children / And it's a hard, and it's a hard, it's a hard, it's a hard / And it's a hard rain's a-gonna fall

And what did you hear, my blue-eyed son? / And what did you hear, my darling young one? / I heard the sound of a thunder, it roared out a warnin' / Heard the roar of a wave that could drown the whole world / Heard one hundred drummers whose hands were a-blazin' / Heard ten thousand whisperin' and nobody listenin' / Heard one person starve, I heard many people laughin' / Heard the song of a poet who died in the gutter / Heard the sound of a clown who cried in the alley / And it's a hard, and it's a hard, it's a hard, it's a hard / And it's a hard rain's a-gonna fall.

Oh, who did you meet, my blue-eyed son? / Who did you meet, my darling young one? / I met a young child beside a dead pony / I met a white man who walked a black dog / I met a young woman whose body was burning / I met a young girl, she gave me a rainbow / I met one man who was wounded in love / I met another man who was wounded with hatred / And it's a hard, it's a hard, it's a hard, it's a hard / It's a hard rain's a-gonna fall

Oh, what'll you do now, my blue-eyed son? / Oh, what'll you do now, my darling young one? / I'm a-goin' back out 'fore the rain starts a-fallin' / I'll walk to the depths of the deepest black forest / Where the people are many and their hands are all empty / Where the pellets of poison are flooding their waters / Where the home in the valley meets the damp dirty prison / Where the executioner's face is always well hidden / Where hunger is ugly, where souls are forgotten / Where black is the color, where none is the number / And I'll tell it and think it and speak it and breathe it / And reflect it from the mountain so all souls can see it / Then I'll stand on the ocean until I start sinkin' / But I'll know my song well before I start singin' / And it's a hard, it's a hard, it's a hard, it's a hard / It's a hard rain's a-gonna fall

OH, WHERE HAVE YOU BEEN, MY BLUE-EYED SON?
OH, WHERE HAVE YOU BEEN, MY DARLING YOUNG ONE?

I'VE STUMBLED ON THE SIDE OF
TWELVE MISTY MOUNTAINS

I'VE WALKED AND I'VE CRAWLED
ON SIX CROOKED HIGHWAYS

I'VE STEPPED IN THE MIDDLE OF SEVEN SAD FORESTS

I'VE BEEN OUT IN FRONT OF A DOZEN DEAD OCEANS

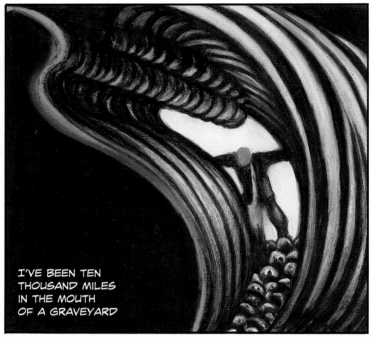

I'VE BEEN TEN THOUSAND MILES IN THE MOUTH OF A GRAVEYARD

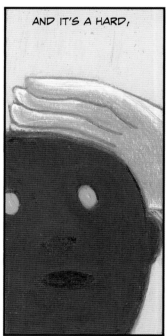

AND IT'S A HARD,

AND IT'S A HARD,

AND IT'S A HARD,

AND IT'S A HARD RAIN'S A-GONNA FALL

OH, WHAT DID YOU SEE, MY BLUE-EYED SON?
OH, WHAT DID YOU SEE, MY DARLING YOUNG ONE?

I SAW A NEWBORN BABY WITH
WILD WOLVES ALL AROUND IT

I SAW A HIGHWAY OF DIAMONDS
WITH NOBODY ON IT

I SAW A BLACK BRANCH
WITH BLOOD THAT KEPT DRIPPIN'

I SAW A ROOM FULL OF MEN
WITH THEIR HAMMERS A-BLEEDIN'

I SAW A WHITE LADDER
ALL COVERED WITH WATER

I SAW TEN THOUSAND TALKERS
WHOSE TONGUES WERE ALL BROKEN

I SAW GUNS AND SHARP SWORDS
IN THE HANDS OF YOUNG CHILDREN

AND IT'S A HARD,

AND IT'S A HARD,

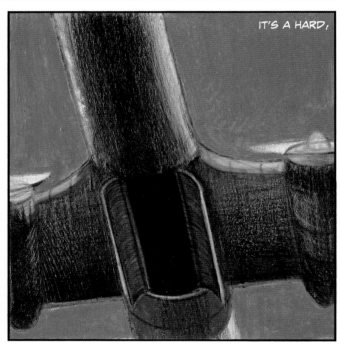

IT'S A HARD,

AND IT'S A HARD RAIN'S A-GONNA FALL

AND WHAT DID YOU HEAR, MY BLUE-EYED SON?
AND WHAT DID YOU HEAR, MY DARLING YOUNG ONE?

I HEARD THE SOUND OF A THUNDER,
IT ROARED OUT A WARNIN'

HEARD THE ROAR OF A WAVE
THAT COULD DROWN THE WHOLE WORLD

HEARD ONE
HUNDRED
DRUMMERS
WHOSE HANDS
WERE A-BLAZIN'

HEARD TEN THOUSAND WHISPERIN'
AND NOBODY LISTENIN'

HEARD ONE
PERSON STARVE,
I HEARD MANY
PEOPLE LAUGHIN'

HEARD THE SONG OF A POET
WHO DIED IN THE GUTTER

HEARD THE SOUND OF A CLOWN
WHO CRIED IN THE ALLEY

AND IT'S A HARD,

AND IT'S A HARD,

IT'S A HARD,

AND IT'S A HARD RAIN'S A-GONNA FALL.

OH, WHO DID YOU MEET, MY BLUE-EYED SON? WHO DID YOU MEET, MY DARLING YOUNG ONE?

I MET A YOUNG CHILD BESIDE A DEAD PONY

I MET A WHITE MAN WHO WALKED A BLACK DOG

I MET A YOUNG WOMAN WHOSE BODY WAS BURNING

I MET A YOUNG GIRL, SHE GAVE ME A RAINBOW

I MET ONE MAN WHO WAS WOUNDED IN LOVE

I MET ANOTHER MAN WHO WAS WOUNDED WITH HATRED

AND IT'S A HARD,

IT'S A HARD,

IT'S A HARD,

IT'S A HARD RAIN'S A-GONNA FALL

OH, WHAT'LL YOU DO NOW,
MY BLUE-EYED SON?
OH, WHAT'LL YOU DO NOW,
MY DARLING YOUNG ONE?

I'M A-GOIN' BACK OUT
'FORE THE RAIN STARTS A-FALLIN'
I'LL WALK TO THE DEPTHS OF THE
DEEPEST BLACK FOREST

WHERE THE PEOPLE ARE MANY
AND THEIR HANDS ARE ALL EMPTY

WHERE THE PELLETS
OF POISON ARE
FLOODING
THEIR WATERS

WHERE THE HOME IN THE
VALLEY MEETS THE DAMP DIRTY PRISON
WHERE THE EXECUTIONER'S FACE
IS ALWAYS WELL HIDDEN

WHERE HUNGER IS UGLY,
WHERE SOULS ARE FORGOTTEN
WHERE BLACK IS THE COLOR,
WHERE NONE IS THE NUMBER

AND I'LL TELL IT AND THINK IT
AND SPEAK IT AND BREATHE IT
AND REFLECT IT FROM THE
MOUNTAIN SO ALL SOULS
CAN SEE IT

THEN I'LL STAND ON THE OCEAN
UNTIL I START SINKIN'
BUT I'LL KNOW MY SONG WELL
BEFORE I START SINGIN'

AND IT'S A HARD, IT'S A HARD, IT'S A HARD, IT'S A HARD
IT'S A HARD RAIN'S A-GONNA FALL

I Want You (1966) interpreted by **Nicolas Nemiri**

The guilty undertaker sighs / The lonesome organ grinder cries / The silver saxophones say I should refuse you / The cracked bells and washed-out horns / Blow into my face with scorn / But it's not that way / I wasn't born to lose you

I want you, I want you / I want you so bad / Honey, I want you

The drunken politician leaps / Upon the street where mothers weep / And the saviors who are fast asleep, they wait for you / And I wait for them to interrupt / Me drinkin' from my broken cup / And ask me to / Open up the gate for you

I want you, I want you / I want you so bad / Honey, I want you

How all my fathers, they've gone down / True love they've been without it / But all their daughters put me down / 'Cause I don't think about it

Well, I return to the Queen of Spades / And talk with my chambermaid / She knows that I'm not afraid to look at her / She is good to me / And there's nothing she doesn't see / She knows where I'd like to be / But it doesn't matter

I want you, I want you / I want you so bad / Honey, I want you

Now your dancing child with his Chinese suit / He spoke to me, I took his flute / No, I wasn't very cute to him, was I? / But I did it, though, because he lied / Because he took you for a ride / And because time was on his side / And because I . . .

I want you, I want you / I want you so bad / Honey, I want you

Bob Dylan © Dwarf Music

Girl From The North Country (1963) interpreted by **François Avril**

Well, if you're travelin' in the north country fair,
Where the winds hit heavy on the borderline,
Remember me to one who lives there.
She once was a true love of mine.

Well, if you go when the snowflakes storm,
When the rivers freeze and summer ends,
Please see if she's wearing a coat so warm,
To keep her from the howlin' winds.

Please see for me if her hair hangs long,
If it rolls and flows all down her breast.
Please see for me if her hair hangs long,
That's the way I remember her best.

I'm a-wonderin' if she remembers me at all.
Many times I've often prayed
In the darkness of my night,
In the brightness of my day.

So if you're travelin' in the north country fair,
Where the winds hit heavy on the borderline,
Remember me to one who lives there.
She once was a true love of mine.

Well, if you're travelin' in the North Country fair.

Where the winds hit heavy on the border line.

Remember me to one who lives there,
She once was a true love of mine.

Well, if you go when the snowflakes storm.

When the rivers freeze and summer ends.

Please see if she's wearing a coat so warm.

to keep her from the howlin' winds

please see for me if her hair hangs long

If it rolls & flows all down her breast.

please see for me if her hair hangs long
that's the way I remember her best.

I'm wonderin' if she remembers me at all

Many times I've often prayed.

In the darkness of my night
In the brightness of my day

So if you're travelin' in the North country fair.

When the winds hit heavy on the border line

the End

Remember me to one who lives there
She once was a true love of mine.

Lay, Lady, Lay (1969) interpreted by **Jean-Claude Götting**

Lay, lady, lay, lay across my big brass bed
Lay, lady, lay, lay across my big brass bed
Whatever colors you have in your mind
I'll show them to you and you'll see them shine

Lay, lady, lay, lay across my big brass bed
Stay, lady, stay, stay with your man awhile
Until the break of day, let me see you make him smile
His clothes are dirty but his hands are clean
And you're the best thing that he's ever seen

Stay, lady, stay, stay with your man awhile
Why wait any longer for the world to begin
You can have your cake and eat it too
Why wait any longer for the one you love
When he's standing in front of you

Lay, lady, lay, lay across my big brass bed
Stay, lady, stay, stay while the night is still ahead
I long to see you in the morning light
I long to reach for you in the night
Stay while the night is still ahead

Lay, lady, lay, lay across my big brass bed
Stay, lady, stay, stay while the night is still ahead
I long to see you in the morning light
I long to reach for you in the night
Stay while the night is still ahead

(The End)

Positively 4th Street (1965) interpreted by **Christopher**

You got a lotta nerve
To say you are my friend
When I was down
You just stood there grinning

You got a lotta nerve
To say you got a helping hand to lend
You just want to be on
The side that's winning

You say I let you down
You know it's not like that
If you're so hurt
Why then don't you show it

You say you lost your faith
But that's not where it's at
You had no faith to lose
And you know it

I know the reason
That you talk behind my back
I used to be among the crowd
You're in with

Do you take me for such a fool
To think I'd make contact
With the one who tries to hide
What he don't know to begin with

You see me on the street
You always act surprised
You say, "How are you?" "Good luck"
But you don't mean it

When you know as well as me
You'd rather see me paralyzed
Why don't you just come out once
And scream it

No, I do not feel that good
When I see the heartbreaks you embrace
If I was a master thief
Perhaps I'd rob them

And now I know you're dissatisfied
With your position and your place
Don't you understand
It's not my problem

I wish that for just one time
You could stand inside my shoes
And just for that one moment
I could be you

Yes, I wish that for just one time
You could stand inside my shoes
You'd know what a drag it is
To see you

You say I let you down

You know it's not like that

If you're so hurt

Why then don't you show it

37

You say you lost your faith

But that's not where it's at

You had no faith to lose

And you know it

I know the reason
That you talk behind my back

I used to be among the crowd

You're in with

Do you take me for such a fool

To think I'd make contact

With the one who tries to hide

What he don't know to begin with

You see me on the street

You always act surprised

You say, "How are you?"
"Good luck"

But you don't mean it

When you know as well as me
You'd rather see me paralyzed

Why don't you just
come out once

and scream it

No, I do not feel that good

When I see the heartbreaks you embrace

If I was a master thief

Perhaps I'd rob them

And now I know you're dissatisfied
With your position and your place

Don't you understand

It's not my problem

I wish that for just one time

You could stand inside my shoes

And just for that one moment I could be

You

Tombstone Blues (1965) interpreted by **Bézian**

The sweet pretty things are in bed now of course / The city fathers they're trying to endorse / The reincarnation of Paul Revere's horse / But the town has no need to be nervous

The ghost of Belle Starr she hands down her wits / To Jezebel the nun she violently knits / A bald wig for Jack the Ripper who sits / At the head of the chamber of commerce

Mama's in the fact'ry / She ain't got no shoes / Daddy's in the alley / He's lookin' for the fuse / I'm in the streets / With the tombstone blues

The hysterical bride in the penny arcade / Screaming she moans, "I've just been made" / Then sends out for the doctor who pulls down the shade / Says, "My advice is to not let the boys in"

Now the medicine man comes and he shuffles inside / He walks with a swagger and he says to the bride / "Stop all this weeping, swallow your pride / You will not die, it's not poison"

Mama's in the fact'ry / She ain't got no shoes / Daddy's in the alley / He's lookin' for the fuse / I'm in the streets / With the tombstone blues

Well, John the Baptist after torturing a thief / Looks up at his hero the Commander-in-Chief / Saying, "Tell me great hero, but please make it brief / Is there a hole for me to get sick in?"

The Commander-in-Chief answers him while chasing a fly / Saying, "Death to all those who would whimper and cry" / And dropping a barbell he points to the sky / Saying, "The sun's not yellow it's chicken"

Mama's in the fact'ry / She ain't got no shoes / Daddy's in the alley / He's lookin' for the fuse / I'm in the streets / With the tombstone blues

The king of the Philistines his soldiers to save / Puts jawbones on their tombstones and flatters their graves / Puts the pied pipers in prison and fattens the slaves / Then sends them out to the jungle

Gypsy Davey with a blowtorch he burns out their camps / With his faithful slave Pedro behind him he tramps / With a fantastic collection of stamps / To win friends and influence his uncle

Mama's in the fact'ry / She ain't got no shoes / Daddy's in the alley / He's lookin' for the fuse / I'm in the streets / With the tombstone blues

The geometry of innocent flesh on the bone / Causes Galileo's math book to get thrown / At Delilah who sits worthlessly alone / But the tears on her cheeks are from laughter

Now I wish I could give Brother Bill his great thrill / I would set him in chains at the top of the hill / Then send out for some pillars and Cecil B. DeMille / He could die happily ever after

Mama's in the fact'ry / She ain't got no shoes / Daddy's in the alley / He's lookin' for the fuse / I'm in the streets / With the tombstone blues

Where Ma Rainey and Beethoven once unwrapped their bedroll / Tuba players now rehearse around the flagpole / And the National Bank at a profit sells road maps for the soul / To the old folks home and the college

Now I wish I could write you a melody so plain / That could hold you dear lady from going insane / That could ease you and cool you and cease the pain / Of your useless and pointless knowledge

Mama's in the fact'ry / She ain't got no shoes / Daddy's in the alley / He's lookin' for the fuse / I'm in the streets / With the tombstone blues

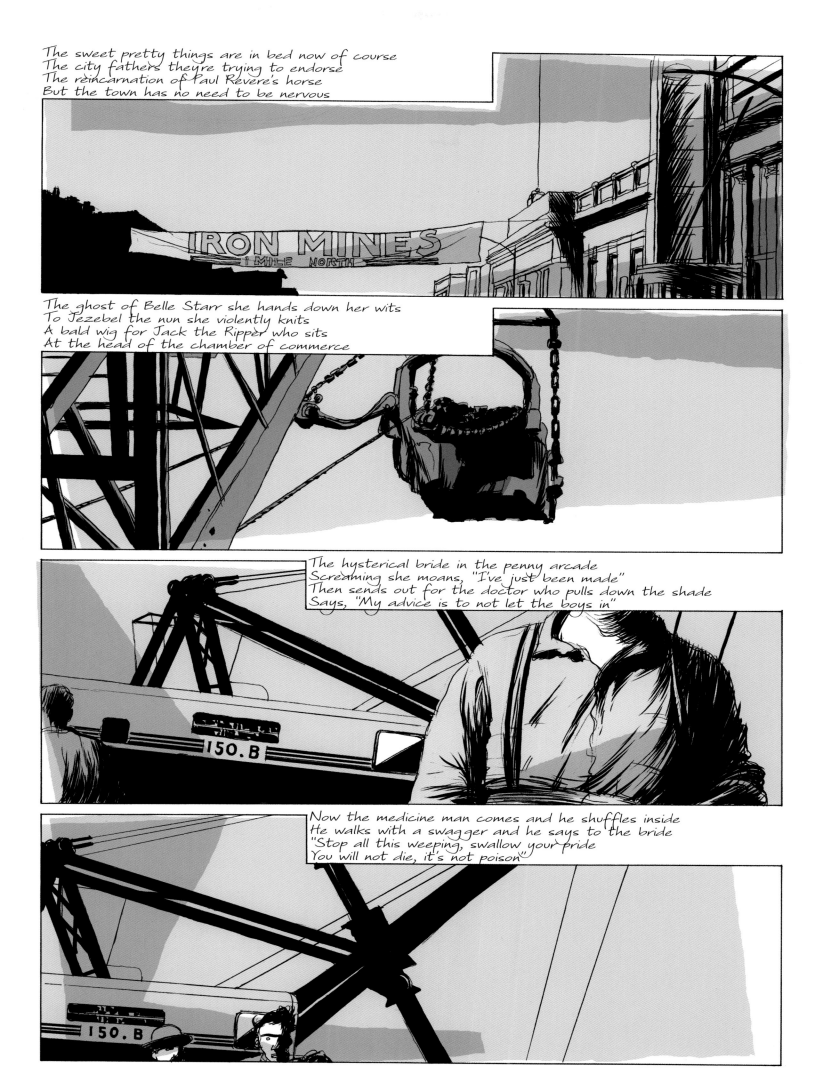

The sweet pretty things are in bed now of course
The city fathers they're trying to endorse
The reincarnation of Paul Revere's horse
But the town has no need to be nervous

The ghost of Belle Starr she hands down her wits
To Jezebel the nun she violently knits
A bald wig for Jack the Ripper who sits
At the head of the chamber of commerce

The hysterical bride in the penny arcade
Screaming she moans, "I've just been made"
Then sends out for the doctor who pulls down the shade
Says, "My advice is to not let the boys in"

Now the medicine man comes and he shuffles inside
He walks with a swagger and he says to the bride
"Stop all this weeping, swallow your pride
You will not die, it's not poison"

Well, John the Baptist after torturing a thief
Looks up at his hero the Commander-in-Chief
Saying, "Tell me great hero, but please make it brief
Is there a hole for me to get sick in?"

The Commander-in-Chief answers him while chasing a fly
Saying, "Death to all those who would whimper and cry"
And dropping a barbell he points to the sky
Saying, "The sun's not yellow it's chicken"

The king of the Philistines his soldiers to save
Puts jawbones on their tombstones and flatters their graves
Puts the pied pipers in prison and fattens the slaves
Then sends them out to the jungle

Gypsy Davey with a blowtorch he burns out their camps
With his faithful slave Pedro behind him he tramps
With a fantastic collection of stamps
To win friends and influence his uncle

The geometry of innocent flesh on the bone
Causes Galileo's math book to get thrown
At Delilah who sits worthlessly alone
But the tears on her cheeks are from laughter

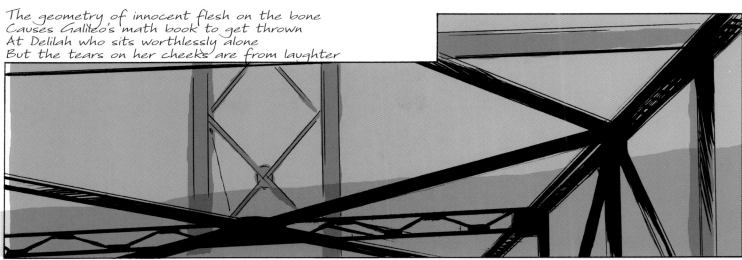

Now I wish I could give Brother Bill his great thrill
I would set him in chains at the top of the hill
Then send out for some pillars and Cecil B. DeMille
He could die happily ever after

Where Ma Rainey and Beethoven once unwrapped their bedroll
Tuba players now rehearse around the flagpole
And the National Bank at a profit sells road maps for the soul
To the old folks home and the college

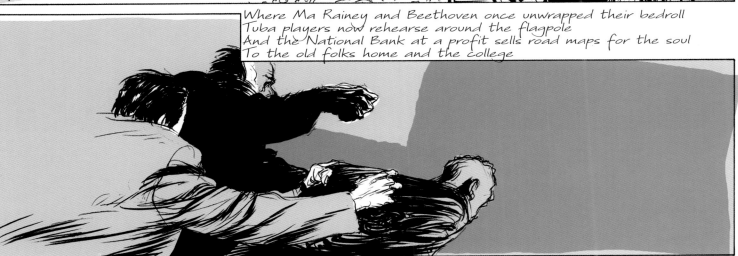

Now I wish I could write you a melody so plain
That could hold you dear lady from going insane
That could ease you and cool you and cease the pain
Of your useless and pointless knowledge

Mama's in the fact'ry
She ain't got no shoes
Daddy's in the alley
He's lookin' for the fuse
I'm in the streets
With the tombstone blues

Desolation Row (1965) interpreted by **Dave McKean**

They're selling postcards of the hanging / They're painting the passports brown / The beauty parlor is filled with sailors / The circus is in town / Here comes the blind commissioner / They've got him in a trance / One hand is tied to the tight-rope walker / The other is in his pants / And the riot squad they're restless / They need somewhere to go / As Lady and I look out tonight / From Desolation Row

Cinderella, she seems so easy / "It takes one to know one," she smiles / And puts her hands in her back pockets / Bette Davis style / And in comes Romeo, he's moaning / "You Belong to Me I Believe" / And someone says, "You're in the wrong place, my friend / You better leave" / And the only sound that's left / After the ambulances go / Is Cinderella sweeping up / On Desolation Row

Now the moon is almost hidden / The stars are beginning to hide / The fortune-telling lady / Has even taken all her things inside / All except for Caïn and Abel / And the hunchback of Notre Dame / Everybody is making love / Or else expecting rain / And the Good Samaritan, he's dressing / He's getting ready for the show / He's going to the carnival tonight / On Desolation Row

Now Ophelia, she's 'neath the window / For her I feel so afraid / On her twenty-second birthday / She already is an old maid / To her, death is quite romantic / She wears an iron vest / Her profession's her religion / Her sin is her lifelessness / And though her eyes are fixed upon / Noah's great rainbow / She spends her time peeking / Into Desolation Row

Einstein, disguised as Robin Hood / With his memories in a trunk / Passed this way an hour ago / With his friend, a jealous monk / He looked so immaculately frightful / As he bummed a cigarette / Then he went off sniffing drainpipes / And reciting the alphabet / Now you would not think to look at him / But he was famous long ago / For playing the electric violin / On Desolation Row

Dr. Filth, he keeps his world / Inside of a leather cup / But all his sexless patients / They're trying to blow it up / Now his nurse, some local loser / She's in charge of the cyanide hole / And she also keeps the cards that read / "Have Mercy on His Soul" / They all play on pennywhistles / You can hear them blow / If you lean your head out far enough / From Desolation Row

Across the street they've nailed the curtains / They're getting ready for the feast / The Phantom of the Opera / A perfect image of a priest / They're spoonfeeding Casanova / To get him to feel more assured / Then they'll kill him with self-confidence / After poisoning him with words / And the Phantom's shouting to skinny girls / "Get Outa Here If You Don't Know / Casanova is just being punished for going / To Desolation Row"

Now at midnight all the agents / And the superhuman crew / Come out and round up everyone / That knows more than they do / Then they bring them to the factory / Where the heart-attack machine / Is strapped across their shoulders / And then the kerosene / Is brought down from the castles / By insurance men who go / Check to see that nobody is escaping / To Desolation Row

Praise be to Nero's Neptune / The Titanic sails at dawn / And everybody's shouting / "Which Side Are You On?" / And Ezra Pound and T. S. Eliot / Fighting in the captain's tower / While calypso singers laugh at them / And fishermen hold flowers / Between the windows of the sea / Where lovely mermaids flow / And nobody has to think too much / About Desolation Row

Yes, I received your letter yesterday / (About the time the doorknob broke) / When you asked how I was doing / Was that some kind of joke? / All these people that you mention / Yes, I know them, they're quite lame / I had to rearrange their faces / And give them all another name / Right now I can't read too good / Don't send me no more letters no / Not unless you mail them / From Desolation Row

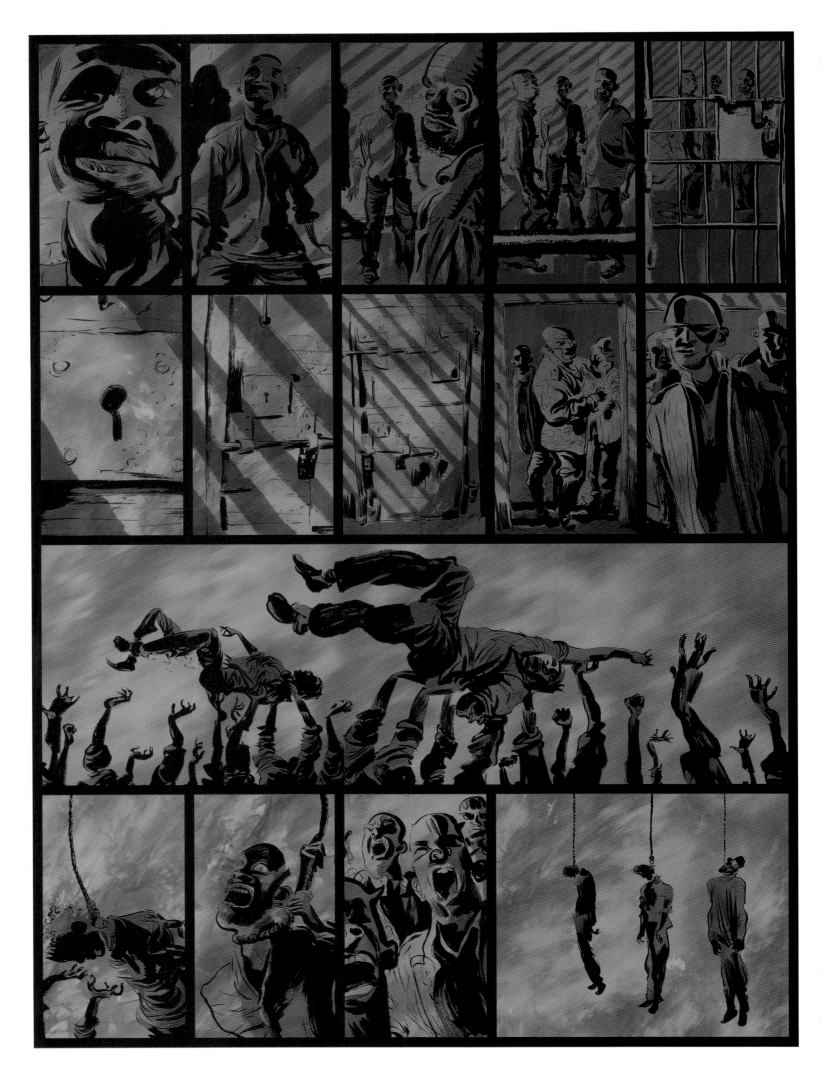

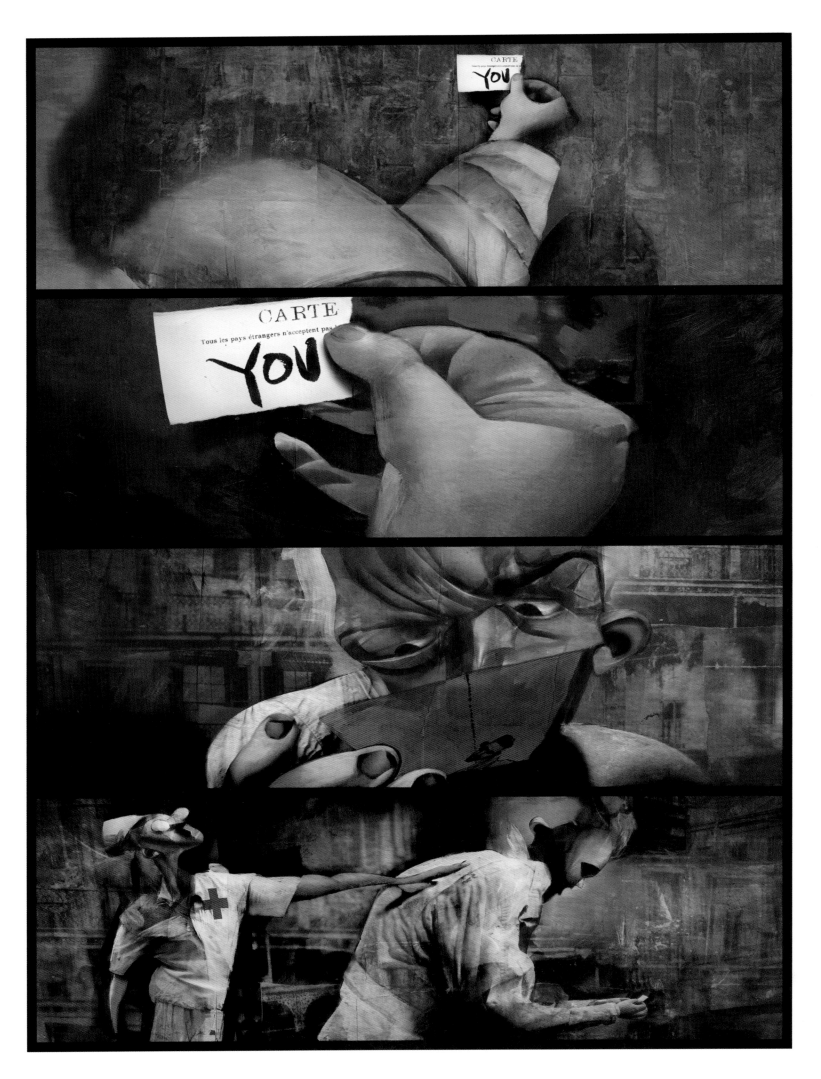

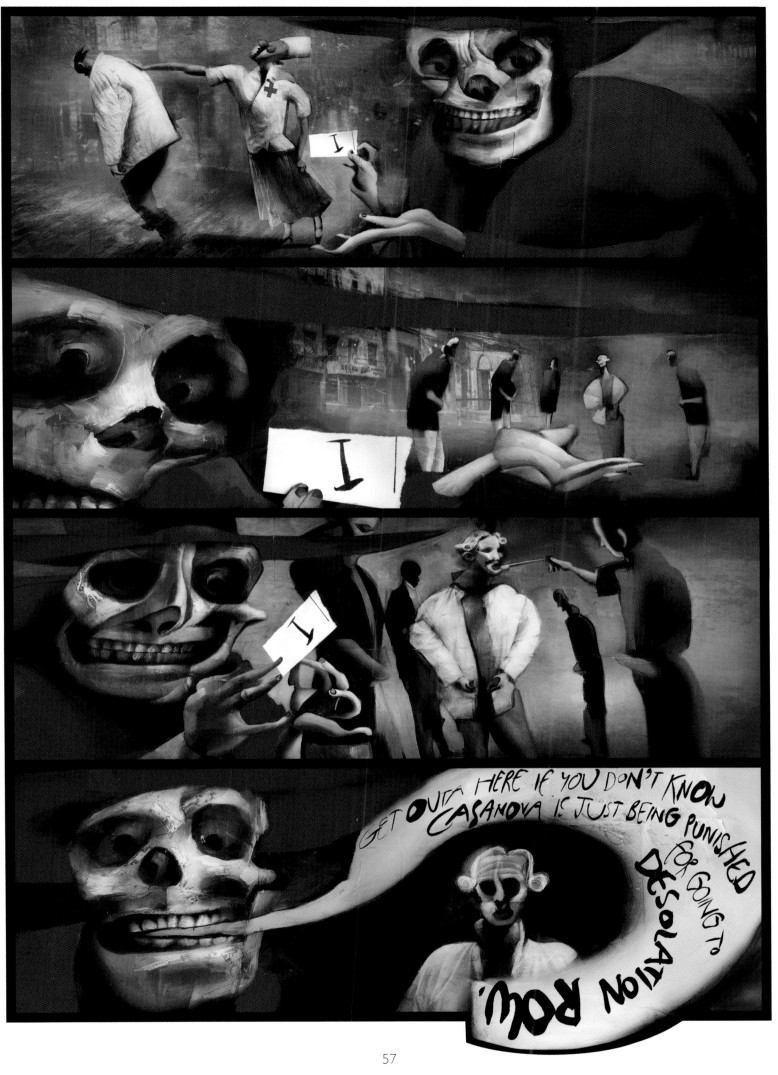

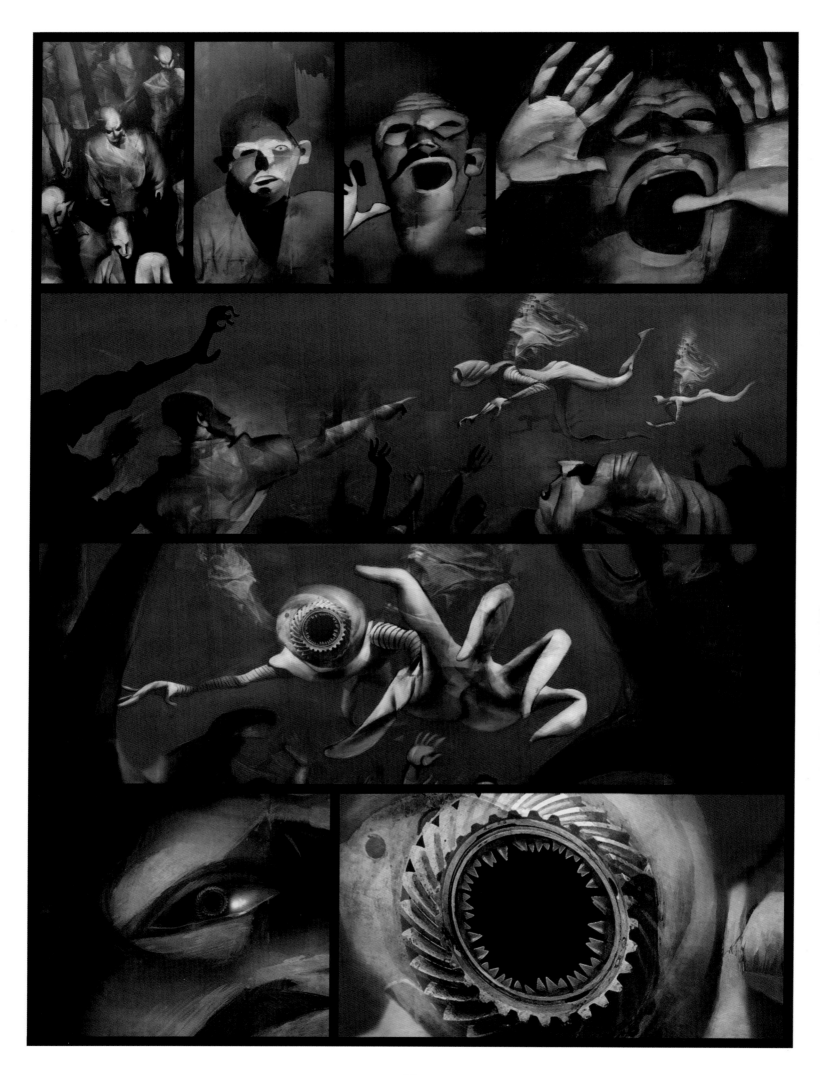

Like A Rolling Stone (1965) interpreted by **Alfred**

Once upon a time you dressed so fine
You threw the bums a dime in your prime, didn't you?
People'd call, say, "Beware doll, you're bound to fall"
You thought they were all kiddin' you
You used to laugh about
Everybody that was hangin' out
Now you don't talk so loud
Now you don't seem so proud
About having to be scrounging for your next meal

How does it feel
How does it feel
To be without a home
Like a complete unknown
Like a rolling stone?

You've gone to the finest school all right, Miss Lonely
But you know you only used to get juiced in it
And nobody has ever taught you
        how to live on the street
And now you find out you're gonna have
        to get used to it
You said you'd never compromise
With the mystery tramp, but now you realize
He's not selling any alibis
As you stare into the vacuum of his eyes
And ask him do you want to make a deal?

How does it feel
How does it feel
To be on your own
With no direction home
Like a complete unknown
Like a rolling stone?
You never turned around to see the frowns
        on the jugglers and the clowns
When they all come down and did tricks for you
You never understood that it ain't no good
You shouldn't let other people get your kicks for you
You used to ride on the chrome horse
        with your diplomat
Who carried on his shoulder a Siamese cat
Ain't it hard when you discover that
He really wasn't where it's at
After he took from you everything he could steal

How does it feel
How does it feel
To be on your own
With no direction home
Like a complete unknown
Like a rolling stone?

Princess on the steeple and all the pretty people
They're drinkin', thinkin' that they got it made
Exchanging all kinds of precious gifts and things
But you'd better lift your diamond ring,
        you'd better pawn it babe
You used to be so amused
At Napoleon in rags and the language that he used
Go to him now, he calls you, you can't refuse
When you got nothing, you got nothing to lose
You're invisible now, you got no secrets to conceal

How does it feel
How does it feel
To be on your own
With no direction home
Like a complete unknown
Like a rolling stone?

1.

1973—

66

3.

4.

5.

2000—

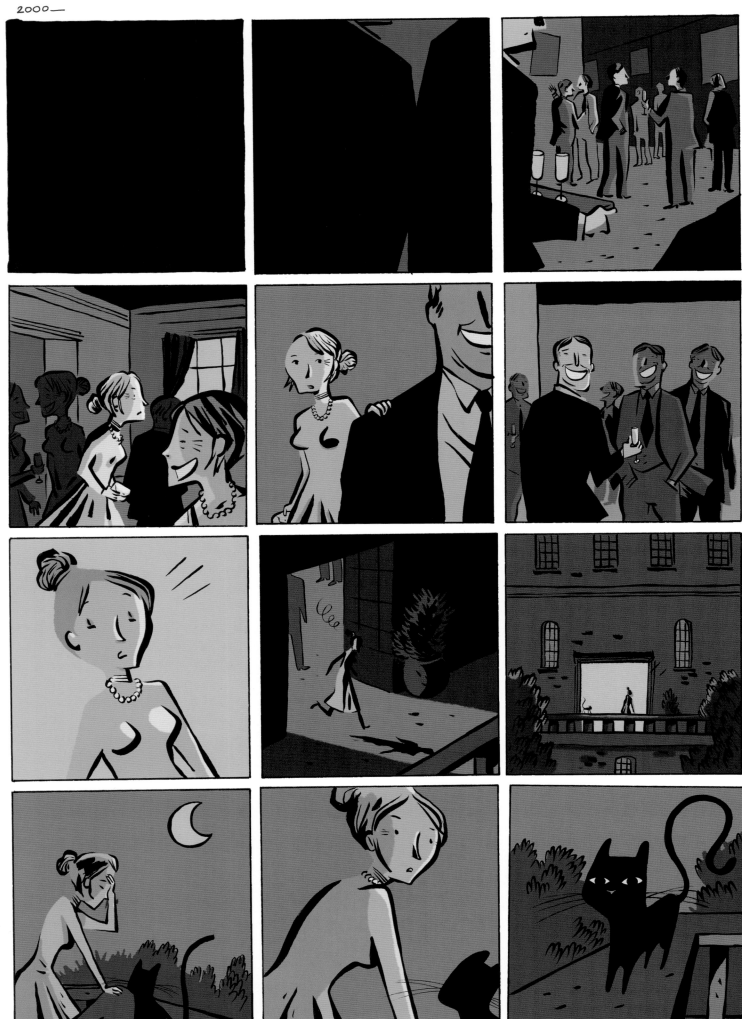

70

2004 —

7.

HOW DOES IT FEEL ?

ALFRED _ RAPHAELLE RIO / MAEL LE MÉE _ HENRI MEUNIER

Hurricane (1975) interpreted by **Gradimir Smudja**

Pistol shots ring out in the barroom night / Enter Patty Valentine from the upper hall / She sees the bartender in a pool of blood / Cries out, "My God, they killed them all!" / Here comes the story of the Hurricane / The man the authorities came to blame / For somethin' that he never done / Put in a prison cell, but one time he could-a been / The champion of the world

Three bodies lyin' there does Patty see / And another man named Bello, movin' around mysteriously / "I didn't do it," he says, and he throws up his hands / "I was only robbin' the register, I hope you understand / I saw them leavin'," he says, and he stops / "One of us had better call up the cops" / And so Patty calls the cops / And they arrive on the scene with their red lights flashin' / In the hot New Jersey night

Meanwhile, far away in another part of town / Rubin Carter and a couple of friends are drivin' around / Number one contender for the middleweight crown / Had no idea what kinda shit was about to go down / When a cop pulled him over to the side of the road / Just like the time before and the time before that / In Paterson that's just the way things go / If you're black you might as well not show up on the street / 'Less you wanna draw the heat

Alfred Bello had a partner and he had a rap for the cops / Him and Arthur Dexter Bradley were just out prowlin' around / He said, "I saw two men runnin' out, they looked like middleweights / They jumped into a white car with out-of-state plates" / And Miss Patty Valentine just nodded her head / Cop said, "Wait a minute, boys, this one's not dead" / So they took him to

the infirmary / And though this man could hardly see / They told him that he could identify the guilty men

Four in the mornin' and they haul Rubin in / Take him to the hospital and they bring him upstairs / The wounded man looks up through his one dyin' eye / Says, "Wha'd you bring him in here for? He ain't the guy!" / Yes, here's the story of the Hurricane / The man the authorities came to blame / For somethin' that he never done / Put in a prison cell, but one time he could-a been / The champion of the world

Four months later, the ghettos are in flame / Rubin's in South America, fightin' for his name / While Arthur Dexter Bradley's still in the robbery game / And the cops are puttin' the screws to him, lookin' for somebody to blame / "Remember that murder that happened in a bar?" / "Remember you said you saw the getaway car?" / "You think you'd like to play ball with the law?" / "Think it might-a been that fighter that you saw runnin' that night?" / "Don't forget that you are white"

Arthur Dexter Bradley said, "I'm really not sure" / Cops said, "A poor boy like you could use a break / We got you for the motel job and we're talkin' to your friend Bello / Now you don't wanta have to go back to jail, be a nice fellow / You'll be doin' society a favor / That sonofabitch is brave and gettin' braver / We want to put his ass in stir / We want to pin this triple murder on him / He ain't no Gentleman Jim."

Rubin could take a man out with just one punch / But he never did like to talk about it all that much / It's my work,

he'd say, and I do it for pay / And when it's over I'd just as soon go on my way / Up to some paradise / Where the trout streams flow and the air is nice / And ride a horse along a trail / But then they took him to the jailhouse / Where they try to turn a man into a mouse

All of Rubin's cards were marked in advance / The trial was a pig-circus, he never had a chance / The judge made Rubin's witnesses drunkards from the slums / To the white folks who watched he was a revolutionary bum / And to the black folks he was just a crazy nigger / No one doubted that he pulled the trigger / And though they could not produce the gun / The D.A. said he was the one who did the deed / And the all-white jury agreed

Rubin Carter was falsely tried / The crime was murder "one," guess who testified? / Bello and Bradley and they both baldly lied / And the newspapers, they all went along for the ride / How can the life of such a man / Be in the palm of some fool's hand? / To see him obviously framed / Couldn't help but make me feel ashamed to live in a land / Where justice is a game

Now all the criminals in their coats and their ties / Are free to drink martinis and watch the sun rise / While Rubin sits like Buddha in a ten-foot cell / An innocent man in a living hell / That's the story of the Hurricane / But it won't be over till they clear his name / And give him back the time he's done / Put in a prison cell, but one time he could-a been / The champion of the world.

Pistols shots ring out in the barroom night

Enter Patty Valentine from the upper hall
She sees the bartender in a pool of blood

Cries out, "My God, they killed them all!"

Here comes the story of the Hurricane
The man the authorities came to blame
For somethin' that he never done
Put him in a prison cell, but one time he could-a been
The champion of the world.

Three bodies lyin' there does Patty see
And another man named Bello, movin' around mysteriously
"I didn't do it," he says, and he throws up his hands

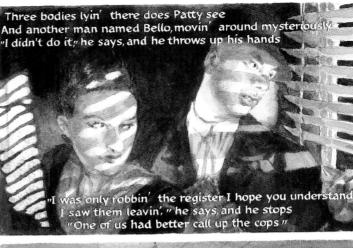

"I was only robbin' the register I hope you understand
I saw them leavin'," he says, and he stops
"One of us had better call up the cops"

And so Patty calls the cops
And they arrive on the scene with their red lights flashin'
In the hot New Jersey night.

Meanwhile, far away in another part of town
Rubin Carter and a couple of friends are drivin' around.

Number one contender for the middleweight crown
Had no idea what kinda shit was about to go down
When a cop pulled him over to the side of the road.

Just like the time before and the time before that
In Paterson that's just the way things go
If you're black you might as well not shown up on the street
'Less you wanna draw the heat.

Alfred Bello had a partner and he had a rap for the cops
Him and Arthur Dexter Bradley were just out prowlin' around

He said "I saw two men runnin' out, they looked like middleweights
They jumped into a white car with out-of-state plates."

And Miss Patty Valentine just nodded her head.

Cop said, "Wait a minute, boys, this one's not dead"

Four in the mornin' and they haul Rubin in
Take him to the hospital and they bring him upstairs.

So they took him to the infirmary
And though this man could hardly see
They told him that he could identify the guilty men.

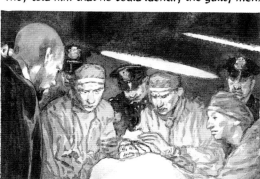

The wounded man looks up through his one dyin' eye
Says "Wha'd you bring him in here for? He ain't the guy!"

Yes, here's the story of the Hurricane
The man the authorities came to blame
For somethin' that he never done
Put in a prison cell, but one time he could-a been
The champion of the world

77

Four months later, the ghettos are in flame
Rubin's in South America, fightin' for his name

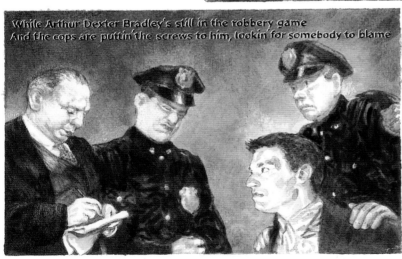

While Arthur Dexter Bradley's still in the robbery game
And the cops are puttin' the screws to him, lookin' for somebody to blame

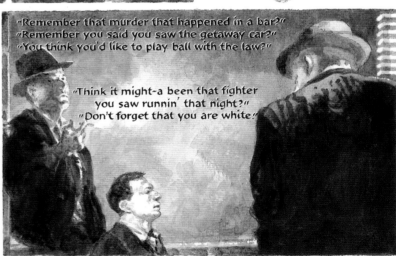

"Remember that murder that happened in a bar?"
"Remember you said you saw the getaway car?"
"You think you'd like to play ball with the law?"

"Think it might-a been that fighter
you saw runnin' that night?"
"Don't forget that you are white"

Arthur Dexter Bradley said, "I'm really not sure"

Cops said, "A boy like you could use a break
We got you for the motel job and we're talkin' to your friend Bello
Now you don't wanta have to go back to jail, be a nice fellow
You'll be doin' society a favor"

That sonofabitch is brave and gettin' braver
We want to put his ass in stir
We want to pin this triple murder on him
He ain't no Gentleman Jim."

35,000

78

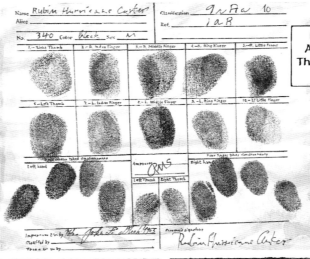

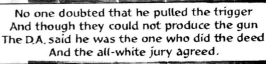

No one doubted that he pulled the trigger
And though they could not produce the gun
The D.A. said he was the one who did the deed
And the all-white jury agreed.

Rubin Carter was falsely tried
The crime was murder "one," guess who testified?

Bello and Bradley and they both baldly lied
And the newspapers, they all went along for the ride

How can the life of such a man
Be in the palm of some fool's hand?
To see him obviously framed

Couldn't help but make me feel ashamed to live in a land
Where justice is a game.

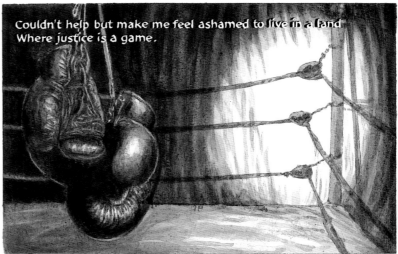

Now all the criminals in their coats and their ties
Are free to drink martinis and watch the sun rise
While Rubin sits like Buddha in a ten-foot cell
An innocent man in a living hell

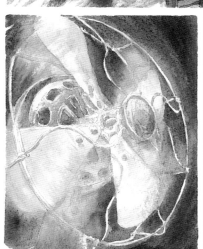

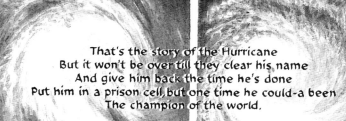

That's the story of the Hurricane
But it won't be over till they clear his name
And give him back the time he's done
Put him in a prison cell, but one time he could-a been
The champion of the world.

Blind Willie McTell (1983) interpreted by **Benjamin Flao**

*Seen the arrow on the doorpost / Saying, "This land is
condemned / All the way from New Orleans / To Jeru-
salem" / I traveled through East Texas / Where many
martyrs fell / And I know no one can sing the blues /
Like Blind Willie McTell*

*Well, I heard the hoot owl singing / As they were taking
down the tents / The stars above the barren trees /
Were his only audience / Them charcoal gypsy maidens
/ Can strut their feathers well / But nobody can sing the
blues / Like Blind Willie McTell*

*See them big plantations burning / Hear the cracking
of the whips / Smell that sweet magnolia blooming /
(And) see the ghosts of slavery ships / I can hear them
tribes a-moaning / (I can) hear the undertaker's bell /
(Yeah), nobody can sing the blues / Like Blind Willie
McTell*

*There's a woman by the river / With some fine young
handsome man / He's dressed up like a squire / Boot-
legged whiskey in his hand / There's a chain gang on
the highway / I can hear them rebels yell / And I know
no one can sing the blues / Like Blind Willie McTell*

*Well, God is in heaven / And we all want what's his /
But power and greed and corruptible seed / Seem to
be all that there is / I'm gazing out the window / Of the
St. James Hotel / And I know no one can sing the blues
/ Like Blind Willie McTell*

well,
I heread the
hoot owl
singing
as they were
taking down
the tents
the stars
above the
barren trees

were his only
audience

them charcoal
G Y P S Y
maidens
can strut
their
feather
well

BUT

NObody
can sing
the blues
like
BLind
Willie
McTell

see
them
big
plantations
burning
hear
the
cracking
of the
whips
smell
that sweet
magnolia
blooming (and)
see the ghost
of slavery ships
I can hear them tribes
a-moaning
hear the undertaker's
bell

yeah
nobody
can
sing the blues
like
Blind willie
McTell

WELL
GOD is in heaven
AND we all
want what's his
BUT

POWER
AND
greed
AND
corruptible
seed
seem to
be all
that there
is
I'm gazing
out
the window
of the
St James
hotel
AND I know
no one
CAN
sing
the
blues
like
BLIND
WILLIE
MCTELL
★

BLIND WILLIE MCTELL
1898 - 1959

BOOTCHILL
RETRO
CHILLOUT

BOB DYLAN
BENJAMIN
FLAO
2008

Knockin' On Heaven's Door (1973) interpreted by **Bramanti**

Mama, take this badge off of me
I can't use it anymore
It's gettin' dark, too dark for me to see
I feel like I'm knockin' on heaven's door

Knock, knock, knockin' on heaven's door
Knock, knock, knockin' on heaven's door
Knock, knock, knockin' on heaven's door
Knock, knock, knockin' on heaven's door

Mama, put my guns in the ground
I can't shoot them anymore
That long black cloud is comin' down
I feel like I'm knockin' on heaven's door

Knock, knock, knockin' on heaven's door
Knock, knock, knockin' on heaven's door
Knock, knock, knockin' on heaven's door
Knock, knock, knockin' on heaven's door

KNOCKIN' ON HEAVEN'S DOOR

SOUNDTRACK BY BOB DYLAN

MAMA, TAKE THIS BADGE OFF OF ME

I CAN'T USE IT ANYMORE.

IT'S GETTIN' DARK, TOO DARK FOR ME TO SEE

I FEEL LIKE I'M KNOCKIN' ON HEAVEN'S DOOR.

Knock, Knock,

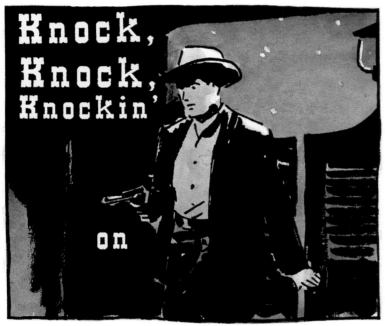

92

Knockin' on Heaven's Door

Knock, Knock, Knockin' on Heaven's Door

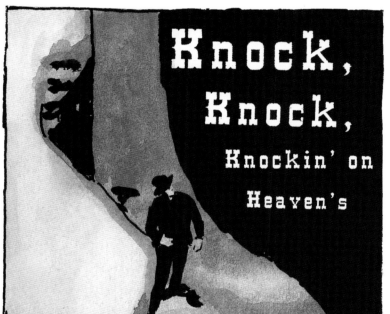

Knock, Knock, Knockin' on Heaven's

Door

Knock, Knock, Knockin'

on Heaven's Door

THE END

Not Dark Yet (1997) interpreted by **Zep**

Shadows are falling and I've been here all day / It's too hot to sleep, time is running away / Feel like my soul has turned into steel / I've still got the scars that the sun didn't heal / There's not even room enough to be anywhere / It's not dark yet, but it's getting there

Well, my sense of humanity has gone down the drain / Behind every beautiful thing there's been some kind of pain / She wrote me a letter and she wrote it so kind / She put down in writing what was in her mind / I just don't see why I should even care / It's not dark yet, but it's getting there

Well, I've been to London and I've been to gay Paree / I've followed the river and I got to the sea / I've been down on the bottom of a world full of lies / I ain't looking for nothing in anyone's eyes / Sometimes my burden seems more than I can bear / It's not dark yet, but it's getting there

I was born here and I'll die here against my will / I know it looks like I'm moving, but I'm standing still / Every nerve in my body is so vacant and numb / I can't even remember what it was I came here to get away from / Don't even hear a murmur of a prayer / It's not dark yet, but it's getting there.

Shadows are falling & i've been here all day
it's too hot to sleep, time
is running away.
feel like my soul has turned
into steel
i've still got the scars
that the sun didn't heal
there's not even room enough to be
anywhere
it's not dark yet,
but it's getting
there.

GASLIGHT CAFE
DAVE VAN RONK
KAREN DALTON
BOB DYLAN

THE F-BEAT SHOP

HOOTENANNY

i was born here & i'll die here
against my will
i know it looks like i'm moving
but i'm standing still
every NERVE in my body
is so
vacant
and
NUMB
i can't even remember
what it was i came here
to get AWAY from

don't even hear a murmur of a prayer

it's not dark
yet, but it's
getting there.

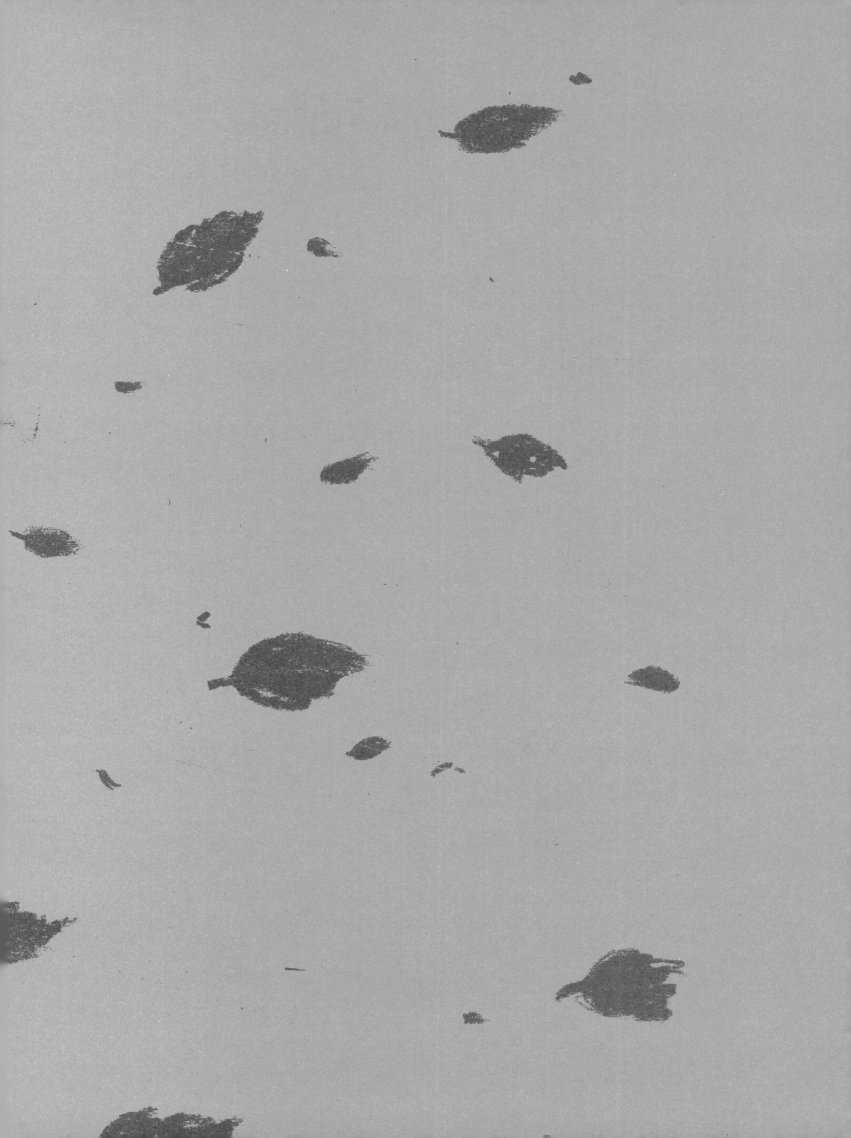